# Wealth Chants

## Chanting Your Way to an Abundant Life

## Elon Bomani

Publisher :

Papyrus Publishing

5680 Hwy 6 #166

Missouri City TX. 459

281.778.9416

Toll Free: 1.888.562.1041

ISBN: 1-9788288-0-1

This publication is designed to provide accu- rate and authoritative information in regard to the subject matter covered. It is sold with the understanding that the publisher is not engaged in rendering legal. accounting, or other profes- sional service. If legal advice or other expert assistance is required, the services of a com- petent professional person should be sought.

# Acknowledgements

I want to extend my most sincere gratitude to several Divas who have helped me with positive feedback on all of my Diva projects. My bestfriend and millionaire dream partner, Ms. Mimi Green, her Diva sister, Ms. Valerie Faust. Also, my Diva confidant, Ms. Akua and my new Diva confidants, Ms. Myrtle Hicks and her lovely daughter Ms. Rhonda Hicks-Smith. You all inspire me and remind me daily of how truly blessed I am to have such good Diva friends.

No Diva could accomplish such feats without the loving support of her family. First and foremost, I want to thank my Divine husband, Benjamin Harrell for his commitment to this wonderful marriage of ten glorious years and helping raise such lovely boys, Rriiver Nyile and Sirius Seven. To my parents, Warren and Pat Ferebee who encouraged me in so many ways but mostly by leading by example. Lastly, but not least, I 'd like to thank my mother, Dr. Nataki Sunsori and my grandmother,Mildred Ferebee "the divas" for being the strong rock that I stand on. I am here because of all of you and the ancestors that came before us all.

Confessions of a Wealthy Diva: A Rich Stay-at-Home Mom

**It's better to be prepared for a miracle and have one, then to have a miracle and not be prepared.**

I needed a miracle and I needed it like yesterday! My worst fears had happened. I was in the mist of a major break-up with my husband. It was on the same scale as one of life's most major domestic battles, The War of the Roses. We had taken our positions. He had his method of defense and I thought I had mine. Like any battle, the main focus is to win the war by any means necessary. He pulled out his major trump card: he emptied "our" joint checking account and transfer "our" income into another account leaving me financially destitute. This was the epitome of emotional and financial abuse. He was the breadwinner and I was the dependent stay-at-home mom—or so he thought.

In order to save my soul and my sanity, spirit said it was time to go-right now! In a matter of minutes, my child and I were poor and homeless. I had to think fast. This was no time to

4

panic. This was a time to pray. The Diva within me was born again. I had turned into the lioness that was determined to protect her cub. I was instructed to use my credit card to stay at a hotel. Go to the yellow pages and call a local woman's shelter. They usually do not take women in unless they were being physically abused. But with the Divine spirit on my side, I mentioned to her I was desperate and was staying at a hotel with my child, and she kindly let me come in. Thank you Maat, and the Placer County Women Center.

With all the spiritual work I had done over the years, I was very clear that this was not about "What my husband did to me". It was about what I was thinking and doing to myself that created this circumstance. The drama Queen in me was healed, I was willing to take full responsibility for were I was at. My husband had to deal with his karma, and that was none of my business. What was my business was to figure out how could I let this happen! I thought I was an independent, strong powerful woman of the new millenium-with a college degree. Obviously, I would not be in such a predicament if that were the case. I had to dig deep to uncover some negative unconscious issues about myself—and quickly.

Like most women, I had a baby. I returned back to run my naturopathic private practice two weeks after giving birth with my baby in tow. I tried everything to make it work. It did not. I had to make a decision. Let some one else raise my child or give up my practice and become a stay-at-home mom. The decision was easy. I could always reopen another practice in the future, but I could not miss out on the once in the life time moments of bonding and growing with my bundle of joy So, I closed my practice and became an at-home mom.

Introspection during a deep meditation revealed to me some startling truths. My father had left my mother to take care of my sister and I. My fear was that my husband would do the same to me. So, I created circumstances to bring my self-fulfilled prophecy to light. Like my mother, I would be a single woman who would have to raise my child alone. Thoughts are very powerful.

Also, I was conditioned by society that money issues, business affairs were handled by men. Even though, I successfully passed several math and science classes, I still believed I was inadequate to handle such matters and nonchalantly passed on the running of my business financial matters to my husband. Furthermore, my husband was in charge of the financial purse strings at home. I was a great healer but not a wise business woman.

Eureka! I got the spiritual message. As a holistic practitioner, I was out of balanced-financially. If you are unbalanced in one area it will have an adverse effect in all other areas of your life-spiritually, physically, and emotionally. I had to get my financial act together for me and my son.

I took charge of my financial life and a miracle has happened! I get to stay at home with my baby and still make a substantial income. I studied the power of money and as a result money and I became friends. In less than one year, I acquired 1.5 million dollars worth of property, brought a house, a car and accomplished my dream of raising a healthy prosperous child while working from home! Not a bad start from someone who started with just $36 dollars in her checking account.

Do you want to know how I did it? Well, here in this book, Wealth Chants, I reveal one of the secrets that help me become wealthy. I develop a wealthy conscious. I was living a poor life simply based upon my thoughts, actions and deeds. So in order to change my life, I did the complete opposite. I started to think, act and do some of the things wealthy people did. To reprogram my mind, I return back to spiritual techniques that help reach the subconscious level of my mind which helps to facilitate a change in the way I performed in life. It has worked for me know let I work for you.

Elon Bomani

**"The Dynamic Diva"**

www.**thedynamicdiva**.com

Check out our website for free e-zine,articles, gifts & much more..

*Nothing is neither good nor bad, only thinking makes it so.*

### Thoughts Are Powerful Things

Here is some food for thought. Eventhough, you cannot hear, see, taste, feel or touch them, thoughts are truly powerful things. They are more real than our five senses. Because you are not aware of this very important discovery, your life may be in a pickle. It is your thoughts that have you in the predicament you are in now. Even if you find yourself doing well, you are more than likely striving to do better. You realize that life is a grand event that you want to be apart of in the most prosperous way! In the universe of abundance, there is plenty to go around. The good news is that you are in the driver's seat and have the freedom to choose your thoughts.

Are you struggling to make ends meet, drama with the family, and having a hard time finding your life purpose? Would you like to be the recipient of more riches in your life: a happy relationship with friends and family; enjoyable job or owner of your own business; and a healthy mind, body and spirit? If so, now is the time to focus on thinking, speaking and acting more positive about all of your life experiences. One thing is very clear, if your spirit drew you to this book then more work needs to be done on you. Otherwise, you would not be reading these words: nothing happens by chance, everything happens for a reason.

Many people are already experiencing the generosity that the Spirit has to offer by chanting their way to abundant living, why not you, too?

# Words Create Your World

The words that you speak daily create the world that you are experiencing. The average person speaks approximately 50,000 words per day. Most of the words spoken are a repeat of what they said the day before, and 97% of the words are negative. If you are like most people, you need more positive, productive, wealthy words in your vocabulary.

It is a scientific fact that when you speak, in order to hear the words, the sound vibrates back to you to give you your voice. So, whatever you say comes back to you. This is called the boomerang effect. Put another way, you reap what you sow. If you speak and hear words of lack and limitation—I'm broke, you make me sick, etc.—the universe will return to you your prayers.

You see, every word that you speak is a prayer. Prayers are our conversation with God. No matter who you are talking to, you are always talking with God. The only true relationship you have in life is between you and the Great Spirit.

So, what have you been saying to God lately? God has given you the free will to choose words that are negative or positive. If you choose positive words, you will have positive experiences. Conversely, if you choice negative words, you will have negative experiences. In essence, you can create your heaven or your hell. It is your choice. This is one of the keys to the secrets of life.

Wealth Chants was created so that you can create the world of abundant living that you desire. The secret is revealed. If you want to live a more fulfilling life, you must think, and speak it into existence. Speak words that empower, motivate and inspire you!

Wealth is more than having money. It means having good health, good relations with family and friends. Wealth is having access to all resources that make way for more joy and peace into your life and makes for a better world for you to live in. For more on this subject refer to Dynamic Diva Dollars at www.thedynamicdiva.com/tools.htm.

Chanting words of wealth will open a window to the subconscious mind to bring into existence your heart's desire. At this level, it becomes a part of your very being and increases your energetic power to the point where you will draw to you positive people, situations and wealth experiences at all times.

Many of my clients who come to me for wealth, health and/or spiritual counseling have been conditioned to believe that their negative experiences are caused by other people, places or circumstances outside of their control. This is not the case. I remind them that it is their thoughts about their experiences translated into words that put them in situations they don't want to be. We tend to give too much power and speak volumes about what we don't want to happen in our lives instead of what we do.

For example, one woman made the claim that all men are "dogs" and she could not find a good man. She held fast to this belief and continued to bash men to her friends whenever she had a chance. Since she was so determined to prove her point, she would always find herself in relationships with "dogs". This is called self-fulfilled prophecy. It was not until she made a conscious effort to change her perception and her dialogue regarding men that her relationships with them changed. If you want your life to change, you are going to have to change the words you use. Remember the saying, think before you speak. You were being put on notice to realize you are responsible for the thoughts you think and once you speak them, the universe will give you the wish that you command.

14

**How to Use this Book to Bring You Wealth Beyond Your Imagination.**

Wealth Chants is your guide to teach you the words and thought patterns that will bring you the enormous amount of wealth that your heart desires. It was created with you in mind. The exercise is simple and requires a good 15 to 30 minutes per day.

The best time to begin is at the most quiet hours between 3am and 6am. This is the time when the divine presence is most available. First, say your morning prayer of abundance and peace. Next, meditate and awaken the spirit within you. Lastly, close your eyes, take a deep breath and open to any page in the book. Whatever page you have attracted to you is the message you need to read. Reflect upon and recite the wealth chant of the day.

Chanting is an ancient spiritual art used by the Africans, East and West Asians and Indians for centuries. Chanting is the act of reciting words repeatedly. Say the wealth chant out loud one hundred times. Then say it silently one hundred times. This should take several minutes. Or you can chant to your hearts content. Once you have completed this exercise at your prosperity alter, you are welcome to have a wealthy day. It is that simple!

If you would like to read the entire book, that's fine too. You may find that you open it to the same page often. This is an issue or subject you need to spend some extra time on. You can use this book anyway you choose for as long as you need to. Just use it. You will get the best results by being consistent and doing the work daily. If you make a valiant effort to change your thoughts and words; fortify them with positive, productive acts, you will, miraculously, start living a successful life. This truth is indisputable.

Keep in mind you are trying to change a powerful force, your mind. It will not happen over night; it may take months or it may take years depending on the amount of time and energy you apply to mastering these skills. In the beginning, you will have challenges with getting rid of negative words and find yourself repeating the words you are trying to release. Old habits are difficult to break. When you say the negative word, immediately state, "cancel universe" and it will be waived. Immediately, replace the word with its positive opposite and all will be well.

Like most treasures, buried deep within everyone is a gift from God cleverly disguised as a natural talent.

God has entrusted within you some God given talents. She has given to you a Gift that can only be expressed by you. Usually the Gift shows up as something you can do naturally without any effort: For instance, you can draw without taking art lessons; you can calculate numbers off the top of your head without the use of a calculator; you can talk to people and help solve their problems better than a psychiatrist. This Gift enables you to lose track of time when you are doing it. You really enjoy it and it makes you feel like you are closer to spirit while you are engaged in it. This is the Gift that you are suppose to share with the world. The beauty of it is that you've been given more than one Gift.The challenge is to figure out which one you want to share with the world first. The ultimate blessing is that you can receive financial reward for sharing your Gift with the world!

Wealth Chant

*I use my God given talents for divine purpose.*

If we were created in the likeness and image
of God why are we acting like paupers?

So many people think that they have to make their sacrifices here on earth in order to receive the riches that "heaven" has to offer. This is one erroneous belief that needs to be dispelled immediately. God wants you to be happy here on earth now. As above so below, is a famous bible term that hits home. The riches of heaven are at your disposal here on earth. You have to believe it and manifest it for yourself. There is no prestige in poverty. When was the last time you saw a homeless person kicking up their heels about his/her life circumstances. Success is your birthright!

Wealth Chant

*I can live a heavenly life here on earth.*

It doesn't take a lot of money to make money.

What was very surprising to the authors of the best seller, The Millionaire Next Door, was that most of the millionaires were self-made millionaires. These people did not come from rich families nor did they inherit large sums of money. They were self-made millionaires that became rich by living below their means, investing in businesses, paper assets, real estate, and accumulated very little debt.

There is still hope for you to do the same. You do not have to make the tired excuse that you need money to make money. Emulate some of the traits of millionaires and soon you will be on your way to making millions.

Wealth Chant

*I am a rich person in progress.*

You are not serving God well dreaming small. If the dream seems enormous and unattainable do it anyway.

We tend to shortchange our blessings when we pray to God for the small things we want in life. We tend to think it is unspiritual to ask God to give us a rich life fit for a Queen. I can remember someone recounting a story about the grace of God. She prayed to God to give her the one dollar she needed to get her grandson a little Christmas gift. She was walking and meditating on this thought and like magic, the dollar appeared before her eyes. She was so excited. I asked how excited would she be if she prayed to God for a million dollars. She stopped, thought and looked at me strange. Trust me God wants the very best for you, for when she created you, she only created the best.

Wealth Chant

*I pray for the wealth that God wants me to have here and now.*

Winners will do whatever it takes no matter what obstacles come their way.

Do you find yourself making excuses as to why you have not lived your dreams yet? Do you feel you need to know more information about the business before you start to do the work? Do you need to go over the numbers again before you buy the property? Are you still lamenting over a childhood experience when someone told you, you could not do "it"? Is the past stopping you from accomplishing your goals?

Winners are faced with as many obstacles as everybody else. Fear of failure is relative. Winners truly understand that the formula to success comes with some trials, setbacks and defeats. Even so, winners win by never quitting and staying-in-the-game. They hold steadfast to their reasons why and know that success is bound to happen-it is just a matter of time.

They will not succumb to any of lifes misfortunes. They are not afraid of the "N"word, NO. Because they know that each NO is bringing them closer to aYes. They keep going and going just like the Ever Ready battery-fixed and focused.

Wealth Chant

*I am winning at the game of Life.*

Money may not be able to buy happiness
but it may buy you peace of mind.

If money brought happiness then Michael Jackson
would be living a charmed life. He has the fame, money
and power, and still one can easily see he is not happy.
Happiness comes from inside you. You will not find it
outside of yourself, or in the material trappings like a
house, car, jewelry and clothes. Start making the decision to be happy no matter what circumstance you find
yourself in. If you are happy without money, you will be
ecstatic when it shows up.

Wealth Chant

*I am a happy.*

Forgiveness opens the floodgates
of abundance to enter your life.


People who have difficulty attracting or keeping money in their lives need to forgive. Forgiveness allows one to open the blockage within our subconscious that occurs from holding on to anger, resentment, and revenge. We do not leave any room for the energy of wealth to enter because the space available is being taking up by negative thoughts. This stops us from receiving our good.

Forgive yourself, your family, your friend, and every circumstance that you thought to be wrong. Holding on to old hurts and pains will leave you sick and impoverished in many ways-lack of money being one of them. A clear forgiving heart and mind will open the way for abundance to enter and guarantee you peace of mind which is worth its weight in gold.




Wealth Chant


*I willingly forgive myself and everyone else.*

Money is an expression of love.

We have all heard the quote, "Money is the root of evil."
With that thought in mind, many of us have steered clear
of money because we fear associating with anything
evil. It is what people do with the money that will determine if it will be for good or for bad. The good of money
have saved many charity organizations, put food on the
table for many people, and paid for operations that have
saved lives. See only the good that money can bring you
and you will see the face of love. From now on, when
you give money (pay your bills) and when you receive
money (receive your paycheck) see it as the symbol of
love. So, how much love do you have, today?

Wealth Chant

*Money is love.*

You are not lacking money.
You are lacking ideas.

If you feel you don't have enough money, it may be because you are not thinking creatively about ways you can manifest more money into your life. This is a true story. Cindy Cashman self-published a book titled, "Everything Men Know about Women", by Dr. Richard Harrison (Cindy's pseudonym). Many women bought this book by the thousands. What made the book a best seller was that all of the 96 pages were blank! Cindy didn't type one single letter! This one idea made Cindy millions and she is retired for life. Each and everyone one of us have a million dollar idea. What is yours? If you don't have a million dollar idea, thinking about one can make one appear. You are only one thought away from your million dollar idea.

Wealth Chant

*I am thinking about my million dollar idea(s).*

Owning a business has tax advantages. With a business, you can take dollars you are already spending and write them off.

If you don't have a home-based business, you need to start one quick! You may be throwing away thousands of dollars. Do you know that you give the government 1/3 of all the money you make over a lifetime? That is a lot of money-which is a good reason why you need to know more about tax avoidance and not tax evasion type of strategies that can help you keep as much of your money in your pocket. Would you give money to the government if you didn't have to? Because of your lack of knowledge about taxes, you may be doing just that. Think about creating a part-time home-based business that will increase your income and talk with a CPA about tax avoidance strategies.

Wealth Chant

*I am going to learn tax advantages that will keep my money in my pocket.*

The learning centers pays me for doing
what I would gladly do for nothing.


I know it is hard to believe, but some people in the world really like the job that they do and would even consider doing it for free! Do what brings you joy. When you love what  you do you will never work a day in your life. In a career that you love, you are doing more than earning money, you are making a difference in the lifes of others. You aren't worried about paying the bills; you become more concerned with the work that will make this world a better place. The paycheck is an added bonus.




Wealth Chant


*I do work that brings joy to the world.*

Do not do a job to just serve yourself,
do a job to serve others.


The people who become massively wealthy at some
point in their lifes worked for free. They worked long tired
hours with very little rewards. And if you ever become
a business owner, you will go from being underpaid, to
barely making it, to becoming grossly overpaid. You will
not be slighted by the Universe for the work you do now;
for if the work is done well, a fruitful harvest will be more
than plentiful in the very near future. If you are working
only for the paycheck, you will only get a paycheck. Be
willing to do the work for free and it will free up opportunities to a live a rich life.


Wealth Chant


*I am willing to work for free.*

Everyone has got to pay their dues.


There are no free lunches in life. Success come with a price. I know it is hard to believe, but there is no simple, "get-rich-quick" way to success: You may have to put in some sweat equity; learn a lot of lessons; lose money; sacrifice your time; and work for free, before you start to reap some rewards. It may not sound very attractive but it is very rewarding.

Wealth Chant


*I am willing to pay the price for my success.*

Do what you love to do, and you
will never work a day in your life.


The next time you look for a job or a business you would like to do, do not focus on how much money you can make. You should choose a job and/or business that will make you happy. Eventhough family and friends will think that you have lost your mind, you may find your true passion and reason for living. Most people are working to take care of their life necessities and they are not happy. They go to work by the tune "I owe, I owe, so off to work I go." They spend a 40 hours a week at this unhappy place. That is a very long time to be unhappy. Especially long, if you don't like what you are doing. It would make the day go by faster and you will happier, if you love what you are doing. You will feel like you are playing at life instead of working at it.


Wealth Chant


*I love the work that I do.*

Find out what you love to do, and then figure out how you can get paid to do it.

There was a man who loved to fly in a helicopter. It was an expensive hobby. He was determined to come up with an idea that would allow him to fly for free and for a living. He found out that his friends wanted to learn how to fly. So, he started a business giving flying lessons. Next, he got the idea to give people tours of the city in a helicopter. To make it more profitable, he hired other helicopter pilots to do the tours and has made a multi-million dollar business out of it. This became very popular and he is making big money doing what he loves to do. What is it that you love to do? Now figure out how you can turn your hobby into a business that you can get handsomely paid to do.

Wealth Chant

*I am creating a business that has purpose and is my passion.*

If you work with a feeling of disdain, you should plan to quit your job and get advice from those who work with joy.

If you find yourself being rude and uncooperative at your place of employment, maybe it is time to let it go. I can remember my job as a hairstylist. I loathed the job and wanted to leave. It finally came to a "head" when I mistakenly colored a woman's hair green and orange. It was a sure sign that I needed to fire myself. When it gets to the point where everything seems to be going wrong at your place of employment, you need to resign and do something better. This is a sure sign you are being put on notice to find your life purpose and not just another job. The thing God had in mind for you to do is available when you make the decision to work for a life instead of a living.

Wealth Chant

*I find work that brings me and others joy.*

Intuition come from the spirit and points
you in the divine direction.

Intuition is the best-kept secret to bring you closer to
your life purpose. We tend to give very little credence
to our intuition because we have been taught to put our
faith in our five senses. Trust your sixth sense. Intuition
is the internal spiritual force that see (feel) things that the
naked eye can't see.  It has the prowess to direct you to
the right circumstance, person, place or thing to bring
you in contact with your life mission.

It is time for you to pay attention to those hunches and
the little voice inside you. Do not rely on your intelli-
gence alone. Your intuition will be there for you when
all else fails.

Wealth Chant

*I put my faith in my intuitive abilities.*

Love the job you have until you get the job you love

It is best to make the most of the career you have and do it with joy even if it is not your life purpose. You can positively prepare for your transition from your present job to your new career by revising your resume, going out on job interviews and network with the people who are doing what you would like to do. And when you are ready to leave, the recommendation from your boss will be easy to acquire because you are leaving on good term for a job well done.

Wealth Chant

*I love my job and the people I work with.*

How many times have you not listened to your inner voice?

I heard it loud and clear as though the Goddess was talking directly to me, "Send the package to Detroit, she will not get it if you sent it to Oakland." I sent the package to Oakland. I rationalized that it was closer and surely she would get it in enough time because the package usually arrives the next day. It did so in all previous occasions and everything worked out fine. My client called, it did not arrive. I knew my error lied in the fact that I did not listen to my spirit. I put faith in man and not in God. I do this spiritual work everyday. I know this stuff, but it is clear I need to do more of the work. So, I paid for it, literally-big time. I had to replace the herbs and used the time I could have spent on other projects redoing the order.

The next time you get a divine thought, trust in your inner voice, it will save you time, money and build your wealth consciousness tenfold.

Wealth Chant

*My inner voice guides me to prosperity.*

Your ideas can make you wealthy.

We are always thinking about great ideas that can make us millions. To our surprise, someone else had copied our idea when we see it on T.V. or heard it on the radio. No one can take from you what is yours. We all live in a great Universe that imparts great opportunity upon us all. There is no impartiality. Someone was given the same idea as you; the only difference is that they acted on it. You don't need to worry. Nothing is lost. You will get another idea. There is plenty to go around. The next time you get that money making idea you better "act like you know" and do it!

Wealth Chant

*I am putting my million-dollar idea in motion today.*

God is always pointing us in the right direction.
The question is are we paying attention.

God is always trying to lead us in the right(eous) direction. We simply are not "paying" attention because we have the audacity to believe that our plan is better or the only way to go. If our plan is so great, why are we in constant worry when we are trying to make our plan work. The truth is, our plan never works, but God's plan always does.

When you want something in your life really bad you have got to surrender it to God and trust that the best outcome is assured. Success does not have to be a struggle. When your spirit is in-charge, you will be given all the instructions, people, places and circumstances to make your efforts appear effortless: your successful business will be born; your real estate will profit;and your health will be restored. You name it, you will get it when you give it up to God.

Wealth Chant

*God gives me all the wealth that life
has to offer and I can handle it!*

Do without doing and know that everything will get done.

Most people think that if they want something done, they have to do it themselves. To a certain extent this is true. God helps those who help themselves. Let's say we tried everything to get the business contract or the job of our dreams and it still has not come to pass. We may want to leave the outcome to divine intervention and pray for some insight. Our power is never enough. We can always use the help of spirit. As we work towards fulfilling our dream, we should give some flexibility to the fact that our way of accomplishing our goal may need some help from a higher source. If it is important to you, surrender it to God and wait patiently.

Wealth Chant

*I leave the final outcome of my life's work up to God.*

When the student is ready the teacher will appear.

Have you ever noticed that when you focus on something important and pay attention to it, it will appear in your life? For instance, you were thinking about calling a friend and the phone rings and it's the friend you were thinking about. Nothing happens by chance. We create all of our experiences with thoughts. So think your way to success. Whatever you focus on, it will grow. If your focus is to acquire a prosperous lifestyle, you will attract people who are prosperous. When you meet that person who is doing what you want to do, ask them for advice. Even better, ask them to be your mentor.

Wealth Chant

*I welcome into my life my prosperity teacher.*

You have got to be a jack-of-all-trades
and a master of some.


You have to be able to do a little of everything in order to get your business or prosperous life off the ground floor. Sometimes you will be the janitor; oftentimes the receptionist; other times the bookkeeper; most of the times, the president; and occasionally the marketing and PR person. You will be surprised at how multifaceted and multi-task oriented you can be when you start small. Most of the greatest leaders, business owner and wealthy people started at very humble beginning before they became a big success and could afford to hire others to do the jobs they once did.

Wealth Chant

*I have the talent and ability to do many task.*

You never have competitors, you always have colleagues.

See everyone you consider your competitor as your colleague. You don't have to compete with them in order to do great business. People who are in the same industry tend to do business in the same areas. They understand that there are many people who have various needs to be met that one group may or may not be able to handle. Go to your local fast food joint and you will see several other fast food companies in the same vicinity. And if you are honest with yourself, you probably have eaten at the other fast food restaurants. No single product is suitable for everyone. People like the choices and usually have more than one favorite. There is plenty of money to go around and share. Major companies know this. You should understand you can create a competitive business and join forces with your so-called competition to make business better for both.

Wealth Chant

*I honor the success of all of my colleagues.*

We all must work for the betterment of each other.

Whatever life path you take, always remember that you are in the business of helping someone. What you do is very important to somebody. If you are a minister, you will heal someone's spirit; if you are a garbage man, you will keep someone's home sanitized; and if you are a mortgage lender, you will help someone buy a house. With each and every one of us doing our part in a small way, we support a harmoniously life for all of us. So, it is important that we show up to do the work well and with the greater human goal in mind of servicing your fellow woman/ mankind. Doing your part to make this world a better place really does matter.

Wealth Chant

*I support every living soul by the work that I do.*

You can have an enjoyable career without sacrificing your morals or your values.

What happened when Enron and other major corporations unveiled the negative side of business, greed and corruption? Lifes were destroyed for the sake of the almighty dollar. A lot of people lost their jobs, many lost their retirement plans and few went to prison.

You cannot live a prosperous life to the extent of lying, cheating or stealing. If you think by stepping on the necks of other people is your road to success, you are sadly mistaken. You will have the money, but will you have the joy of a job well done? A true professional will not compromise her morals and values for financial gain.

You should conduct business each day with the utmost integrity. The word will spread and more people will want to do business with a person they trust and respect. Moreover, you will feel good at the end of the day knowing you have made a positive difference in the lives of others and set standards that they can follow.

Wealth Chant

*I am moral and ethnical about how
I conduct my business affairs.*

What you see in someone else lies
within you. We are all connected.

You know how truly rich a person is by the friends he or she has. She has been endowed with the love of others because she has the ability to see the best in most people she interacts with. She realizes that all human beings regardless of race, creed, color or religious affiliation want to be honored, cherished, respected, and loved for who they are. Everything in her life comes from a place of love, and only need a loving response: anything less than that will show up in her life as not real. She understands this fact to be the truth for her and everyone else.

Wealth Chant

*I honor all of my loved ones, friends and associates.*

True success is accomplish at the expense of keeping your morals and values intact.

When you have to sell your soul to make a lot of money, you will pay an even bigger price with your conscious. We all have talents we've never fully explored, abilities we could put to use in new ways.

You don't have to get to the "top" by forsaking your morals and values. Many people make excuses for people who appear to achieve success unethically. Some even try to emulate their way of doing business. It has become a normal practice to lie, cheat and steal for money. The only problem is that at the end of the day, you will have to look at the woman in the mirror. You will have to be the one to answer to a higher spirit when the Day of Judgment comes life.

Wealth Chant

*I use my God given talents to make this world a better place.*

Talented people can do many talented things.

As the old adage goes, "if at first you don't succeed, try, try, and try, again." I am amazed that many people think that a multidimensional spirit would be so stingy and give them only one talent to succeed. You were endowed with a multitude of talents and the resources to make it big in the world. If one business doesn't go according to plan, try another one. Your success is one business venture, one talented idea or one investment away.

Wealth Chant

*I am willing to try another way
to achieve massive success.*

The next time you pay your bills do it cheerfully. You were blessed with money before you could afford it.

Many moons ago, I can remember angrily paying my bills wanting to say very salty words to (before my spiritual days) the lender for sending me the bills in the first place. Didn't he know I was low on cash and I could barely afford to make the payments? First of all, the lender didn't beg me to open the credit card account. Nor did he coerce me to spend money on the credit card. Moreover, he didn't have to extend to me the favor of giving me a card. It is not the lenders fault. Bills aren't here to hurt us. They are here to remind us that we have an abundance of friends who feel we are worthy of lending money to. And if we respect the money that was loaned to us and return it with cheer, we can use other people's money to buy a house and a business that will increase our asset and lead us to a more prosperous lifestyle.

Wealth Chant

*I pay my bills cheerfully and bless my lenders.*

You cannot see your face in running water.

*African Proverb*

How can you think of that great million dollar idea if you are talking all the time, busy watching T. V., listening to the radio, fussing with the children, reading the newspaper, gossiping with your friends, working from sun up to sun down, dining out, sleeping to the sounds of Bach, or e-mailing your clients. Stop the madness! If your mind is busy with too many thoughts, it cannot bring you the thoughts that can change your life forever. You must sit down, get very quiet, close your eyes and meditate. And in the stillness, you will find your truth. Your wealthy idea is only a thought away.

Wealth Chant

*I claim a prosperous idea.*

Have your money work for you
instead of you working for your money.

Residual income is money that you make on a continual basis from a onetime effort. Another way of putting it, residual income allows you to make money while you are asleep. If you write a book, sing a song, produce a movie, you get royalties (a form of residual income). James Brown still gets royalty checks from his 60's song, "I Feel Good". Elvis's estate is still bringing in millions of dollars a year even though the king is dead. Another source of residual income can be acquired while investing in the stock market known as dividends. Additionally, residual income can be made on the internet. Residual income has been the bread and butter of multi-level and network marketing business for years. Lastly, residual income can be obtained from rental properties that yield positive cash each and every month. Residual income is the true way of acquire wealth and not money. You need to make sure that residual income investments are apart of you financial portfolio if you want to acquire true riches.

Wealth Chant

*I am making more money using*
*very little of my time and efforts.*

Your failures in life come from not realizing your nearness to success when you give up.

*Yoruba proverb*

If you talk to many of the successful, wealthy people, each will tell you that success or money didn't come to them overnight. It took a lot of trial and error to climb the ladder of wealth. They will emphasize that just when they thought they should give up— throw in the towel— is when they had a major breakthrough. Nothing worthwhile comes easy. If it did everyone would be rich. Whatever you do, do not quit. Stay in the game and something great is bound to happen.

Wealth Chant

*I do not recognize failure and failure does not recognize me.*

A banker is someone who charges you
high interest to borrow someone else's money.

Why do we continue to put our money in a bank savings account when it will earn less than 2% interest? Why do we put our money in a bank that charges us a fee to open a checking account? Moreover, why do we put our money in a bank that declines our loan request even though we are fully qualified? It is time to shop around for a bank or other financial institutions that will honor our money and help us to make more of it. If they cannot help you make your money grow, you are going to have to let them go!

Wealth Chant

*I will bank where I am honored.*

# Silence is Golden.

There are some things you tell somebody, some things you tell nobody, and some things you tell everybody. The wisdom is in knowing the appropriate time to speak about your good and when not to speak. To be safe, err with caution. When something really means the world to you, share the thought (s) with God.

If it is a great business idea or a dream vacation, do not let anybody breathe on your fantastic idea or goal. So many people would not understand and think thoughts that may cancel out your wishes. The divine will keep it safe. You don't have to worry about negative energy counteracting your efforts. Sometimes it is good to speak only to the still voice within and know that that is enough.

## Wealth Chant

*I silently bring my prosperity goals to life.*

Poor people think poorly and this is
the main reason why they are poor.


If your thoughts about money are poor, poverty will be a way of life for you. If these words sound familiar to you, this could be the reason why money is acting like a distant cousin. If you want more money in your life, it is so important that you stop thinking and talking negative about your money problems: "A day late and a dollar short"; "I never have enough money"; "I am broke"; "I always run out of money"; and "Where does all my money go?"

Like the biblical phrase states, "Life and death is in the power of the tongue." You can give life to your money dreams or your dreams about money can die a slow death if you speak negatively about the things you want. You are wise to claim the good that money can do for you. Money will not intimidate you if you develop a positive relationship with it. If you honor money, money will honor you with its presence.


Wealth Chant


*I have more than enough money in my life.*

When you are employed by God Inc.
you never worry about unemployment.


Put God at the center of your career goals and you will never have to worry about whether the job is right for you or is your divine purpose. God will not lead you in the direction that won't compliment the skills you already process. It is important for you to trust in the Universe to lead you on your journey. Look at it this way, you have tried it your way and it has got you here. If your financial affairs are in bad shape, you definitely need to seek out your higher calling. If your financial affairs are good, it can only get better when you let God take over.

Wealth Chant

*I trust in God to show me the*
*way to my divine purpose.*

With money a dragon, without money a worm.

*Chinese proverb*

A lot of benefits are established when people acquire money and a wealthy lifestyle. They are free of money worries. They are more confident and self-assured. Everyday is filled with new possibilities. They feel empowered and love life. All of their basic needs are met and now they can focus their time and energy on fulfilling their dreams, as well as the dreams of family, friends, and associates.

Wealth Chant

***I am free to be me.***

Do the act and the money will follow.

Mother Theresa served the poor without asking for financial compensation all her life. She did a lot of good for many people. When she was eulogized, they didn't talk about how much money she had in her bank account. They spoke about the rich life that she lived serving people and how it impacted not hundreds but millions of people to do the same all over the world. One good act by one person can affect the actions of millions to do the same.

Wealth Chant

*My wealth serves mankind.*

To experience prosperity from the heart,
you do not need money or possessions.


The good thing about living a prosperous life is that you do not need any money to start. A prosperous life begins by thinking prosperously. You have no fear. You are in a place of love and are willing to share it with the world. Life itself brings you enormous joy. You feel blessed everyday and see the magic that unfolds by your presence.

Wealth Chant


*I live a prosperous life.*

Just show me the money tree and
I'd be happy to pick you a few dollars.


When children are young teach them the value of money. They do learn very early in life that it takes money to bring them their hearts desire. Give them a budget; teach them to save 50% of their allowance. Teach them to buy items they need first and wait until they have extra funds for extravagant items or teach them to live a simple life with very little wants—a hard task to follow at a young age. Most important, children learn about money by—example, so practice what you preach.

Wealth Chant

*I share my wealthy wise ways with my children.*

If money talks then mine sounds like a whisper.

I think that most people who complain about money think that by complaining, money will somehow show up. Complaining about money will only keep money away. If your money is funny, you need to do something constructive to bring more of it into your life. Take money management classes (some are free). Read magazines and books about money. Talk to people at your bank about money—how you can learn about money and how it can work better in your life. I am learning new money ideas daily.

Wealth Chant

*I am learning new money ideas daily.*

A little rain each day will fill the river to overflowing.

*Liberian proverb*

Saving for a rainy day is so important, especially since, you know it will rain. You will get rid of the nagging worry about the rainy day by putting money in the bank or an investment vehicle that will help it multiply. When that day does come, it will not be a sad day, but a happy one because you have in place the resources to make the clouds of debt go away and make room for the sunshine of wealth to come out to play.

Wealth Chant

***Patiently, I am saving money so that money will overflow in my life.***

The fool is thirsty in the mist of water.

You always hear people say, "I don't have any money?" How can you be poor when money is surrounding you wherever you go? It is at the bank. It is on Wall Street. It is available to you in so many ways through inheritance, loans, grants and credit. Money is in abundance. It is not impartial nor given to a selected few. It can be easily transferred to you once you choose to welcome it in your life. Anyone can acquire money.

Wealth Chant

*Money is coming to me through various sources.*

With money in your pocket you are wise,
you are handsome and sing well, too.

*Yiddish proverb*

Don't let your ego get the best of you when you acquire money. If you are humble about your money gains, it will open up doors that will bless you with the resources to bring to you your heart's desire. When money comes into your life so do the people, situation and circumstance to test whether or not you can handle money well. Be careful. People will claim to help you. In reality, they maybe try to help themselves to your money.

Wealth Chant

***A draw to me financial advisors that have my best interest at heart.***

Sometime you cannot find love in a gift.

"Deck the halls with bells and holly, fla,la la,......... it's the holiday season again. The spirit of Christmas and other holidays are lost among the commercialism. The gift of giving has given way to the stress of spending money on credit cards that you know you don't have nor can afford. You are rushing to finish a shopping list of gifts that will be forgotten in the coming years or sold at next year's garage sale. No one is talking about the spirit of the holidays. Many are trying to get through the holidays with some form of peace of mind. Let's return back to the spirit of holidays giving by using our money for the good of spirit. Give to a spiritual/religious organization that sends the energy of love via the change in your pocket. If you don't have the money, volunteer your time which is sometimes more powerful.

Wealth Chant

*I give the gift of love this holiday season.*

A single conversation across the table with a wise man is worth a month's study of books'
*Chinese Proverb.*

Find a mentor. It will save you tons of money on books, tapes and seminars. Whatever it is you want to do, find someone who has already accomplished your goal. Take them out to lunch and ask them their personal secrets. People love to be admired and many love to share the information because they truly feel good about what they have accomplished. I remember talking to a millionaire investor. Since he didn't have to be at work, he gave me many tips during our hour-long conversation. He saved me hundreds of dollars during that one conversation. He told me he understands that in this world there is only abundance and if he wanted more to come to him he was going to have to share the information. You have something to share with the world. Give to someone without trying to get paid to do it-at least some of the times.

Wealth Chant

*I welcome a mentor in my life.*

You best investments are not found in real estate, the stock market or the lottery. You best investment is in God.

The greatest investment we could make is our investment in our faith, family and finances.

Faith is knowing that the divine spirit has your best interest at heart and want you to be happy in ways that will bring peace to you and your family. Family is those who will sustain you, support you and be your inspiration as you strive to acquire a rich life. The finances will come once you handle life in that order and not in the reverse.

Wealth Chant

*I'm investing in my Faith, first; my Family, second; and my Finances last.*

When one door closes, another door opens.

Never worry about one business failure. Get right back into the game and find another business. This one didn't work out but another one will. Learn the lessons from your mistakes and move on to the next wealth opportunity. Almost all of the successful millionaires failed at their first attempt. The universe will provide you with another opportunity.

Wealth Chant

*I work in harmony with universal laws and principal.*

You can never save any money if you
are always spending money.

The more money you spend, the more you will have to work in order to bring it back into you life. Saving money will give you the security of knowing you do have money readily available. It is wise to save up three months of your salary for the rainy days. Put it in a money market account that will bear some interest and forget about it until the rainy day comes.

Wealth Chant

*I release my old spending habits
and adopt new saving habits.*

What things so ever ye desire when ye pray, believe that ye receive them and ye shall have them. *Mark 11:24*

You have got to believe it before you see it.  God is good and very generous. You have got to have the courage to dream big and ask for divine guidance to bring to you what you want.

Wealth Chant

*I believe that I will receive the*
*good that the spirit has to offer.*

You  block your blessing when you refuse to receive.

If there is anything women have a challenge with in balancing their lives, it is the dichotomy of giving and receiving. Now, I think, the giving part, we got it down. We will give to the point of no return- and that is usually what happens-we do not receive. And because we deny the gift of receiving, we become resentful and feel we are being taken for granted. But when someone wants to return a favor or a kind gesture, we say no. This is a big mistake according to natural law. When you refuse to receive, even a compliment, you cut off your blessings. In order for your life to flourish, you must allow the cycle of giving and receiving to play itself out. Giving should be something we do because we want to, not because we are women and. It's the right thing to do.

Wealth Chant

*I delete practice the art of giving and receiving!*

One must realize that all who have accumulated great fortunes did a lot of dreaming, hoping, wishing, desiring and planning before acquiring money.

Most of the successes experienced by the wealthy started as a dream. They took that dream and gave it life. Money was the end result of all the hard work, dedication and sacrifices. Great fortunes don't just show up. It requires the very best of you and you will be better for it in the end. You have to keep this truth in mind as you strive towards your dreams. Do not become a millionaire for the sake of becoming a millionaire. Do it to see what it will make of you. There are so many good life lessons that can be learned; like determination, perseverance, patience, tenacity, courage and faith, just to name a few. Give yourself the opportunity to see your greatness at work.

Wealth Chant

*I am planning, hoping dreaming and*
*preparing for my great fortune.*

In order to be successful in the world of Business you have to pray, fast and meditate.

Prayer allows us to connect to the source of our greatest power. Meditation allows the source to give direction as to how to best utilize the power. Fasting gives us spiritual food to cleanse the body so that we have the capacity to physically put the power in motion. Prayer, meditation and fasting will bring you into alignment with your magnificence and instill the forces needed to handle any business initiative.

Wealth Chant

*I pray, fast and meditate my way to a prosperous life.*

Money is magnetic.

Money is made up of energy. If you want more money in your life you have got to attract it by creating various opportunities for it to enter your life. How about starting or buying a business, creating an investment club or REIT, buying real estate or having a garage sale. Try to figure out creative ways to draw more money in your life. It not enough to request it presence, you must find a way to make it come into your life and stay around awhile by developing concrete investment vehicles that will allow it to grow and grow and grow.

Wealth Chant

*I attract money to me via various sources.*

In order to prosper, you must feel you deserve to prosper.

It is your birthright to be prosperous. You must know this and believe this fact before you begin your journey on acquiring wealth or you will surely fail no matter how much money you acquire. It is an attitude. It is so important that you develop the confidence and courage to accomplishing all of your financial dreams. You have to believe with all your heart that you deserve to live a rich life.

Wealth Chant

*I deserve to be prosperous.*

# Women dictate the economy, but why do we let men rule it?

Women who are financially challenged tend to have low self-esteem. Most women who don't feel that they are'"worth" anything tend to be broke and delegate their money to their husband, the government, the job or even worst their financial planner. They are still looking for prince charming to take care of them financially.

Well, ladies your prince has turned into a frog. It is more paramount today for women to take control of their financial purse. Statistically wise, 50% of marriages end in divorce and the woman's income can drop on average 73%. Moreover, 7 out of 10 women will live in poverty and be left with the responsiblity to financially fend for themselves. As daunting as this may appear, there is still much hope for women. If you financially educate yourself, you can build a wall of confidence and high self-esteem about money issues. It is now time to for woman to be comfortable with being financially astute.

Wealth Chant

*I manage my money well.*

# Wealth is a wealth does.

You are not going to get your financial act together overnight. You have the rest of your life to get this money management system down. You should focus on taking one day at a time. Do something each day that will get you a little closer to economic freedom and independence. You can read financial books, magazine, and news articles. You can have a garage sale and put the savings in a money market account or pay down on a credit card bill. You can journal your experiences daily. All of these actions are powerful progressive steps that will help you to accomplish your goal. Be patient, consistent and discipline. If you backslide and pick up a spontaneous item that is not in the budget, do not beat yourself up. Think about why it happened. Was it because of habit or an emotional impulse? Next, make it your goal to cut down on spur of the moment buying. This is truly a good thing because now you are becoming conscious of your destructive money habits and know what to do to minimize them.

## Wealth Chant

*I am acquiring wealth one day at a time.*

Can you give me back my time?

If you have to choose between money and the time spent with your children, the latter is more precious. No amount of money can substitute experiencing your child's first smile, taking their first step and saying their first words. Time goes by so quickly in a child's life; do not miss out on it. Money can always be made, but the time lost from spending quality time with the one you love can never be replaced.

Wealth Chant

*I make time for my children and family.*

The more you seek the goddess of Knowledge, the more the Goddess of wealth will seek you.
*Ancient India Spiritual Master.*

Did you know that many people who become instant winners of the lottery end up broke or bankrupted in a couple of years. That is not surprising because when one has a poverty consciousness, no matter how much money they make, they will subconsciously create poverty experiences again and again. Their lack of knowledge about money and how to manage it creates a poor lifestyle for them. Their outward financial circumstances may have changed but the inner thought and conditioning made money stayed the same. If you want your life to change, you have to change your vibrations. You and money have an energy connection. Wealth is something that one acquires when they intellectually understand  and intuitively develop it. The knowledge of how to budget, create a spending plan, investigate various investment vehicles and tax strategies will create circumstances that will bring wealthy experiences. A good financial education and an abundance building attitude will give you the knowledge to become financially secure.

## Wealth Chant

*I welcome the Goddess of knowledge in my life so that I can develop a friendship with the Goddess of wealth.*

It is not rocket science. If you think, act
and do wealth, you will be wealthy.


You don't become wealthy or prosperous when the money shows up. The money shows up when you think and act like you are in a state of abundance. Wealth is developed from within. Oprah grew up poor but she never thought poorly of herself. And because of that small but major truth, she is richer than many people who were born into money.

Wealth Chant

*I believe that I live an abundant life now.*

The greatest gift that family and friends can give you during the holiday season is the gift of understanding.

How many holidays are in a year? There are about 15 holidays people celebrate each year-Christmas, Easter, Valentine, and Halloween are just a few of them. If you are spending money on every single holiday, you are going to have difficulty amassing a fortune. Holidays are Holy days but the meaning has been lost and replaced by commercialistic acts called gift giving. Get back into the meaning of spreading love and cheer. It will relieve the stress of spending money you do not have and buying gifts that will be sold at the next garage sale by the person you gave it to. It's a lot cheaper and truly priceless to express the gift of love.

Wealth Chant

*I celebrate all holy days with the gift of love for all family and friends.*

You are in the business of giving love and serving your follow man and womankind in some grand way.

Love truly makes the world go round. Love is what we are made of. No matter what kind of business you are engaged in, say a silent prayer for each person you meet and always see the divinity in him or her. It helps you to conduct business with the utmost integrity and encourage doing a good job. What better way to serve the god and goddess in each person that you come in contact with. In a loving environment wealth will flourish.

Wealth Chant

*I send love and light to people I come in contact with.*

Joy has no cost.
*A course in Miracles.*

Do what brings you joy and you will never work a day in your life. Work that brings you joy will have you up early in the morning, and going to bed late at night with a smile on your face.

Wealth Chant

**I am the joy I am seeking.**

Let's start giving more rather than focus on receiving more.

Why do you work? Do you work to pay the bills-make ends meet? Do you work because the job is prestigious? Do you work because your parents think it is the best job for you? If any of these statements hits home, your life's work is not getting done. When you do the work you love, you are in a place of joy and peace. People who interact with you get the benefit of a job well done. You get the blessing of giving your very best product and service-line.

Wealth Chant

*I am motivated to spread love.*

Poor people live a bankrupted life.

Poor people want a way out. Unfortunately, many don't know how to find the way. The only way to get out of their predicament is to do something different when they receive the cash. Many would like a big break and are willing to work for it if they just knew how. If you think you are poor, start to think rich. Then go about the business of investigating how you can attract more money in your life. It does not cost anything to go to the library and read about the wealthy. There are government programs to help you get a job, housing, and create a business. There are always free courses on money topics listed in the newspaper.

You have the be the aggressor. Money is not going to come looking for you. You have to go about the means of finding money. And with your newfound knowledge about money will open up many venues to bring financial opportunities to you. And once money shows up in your life, you will know exactly what to do to keep the money and make sure it does not disappear like magic.

Wealth Chant

*I relinguish my poor thought pattern*
*and replace it with rich ideas.*

People are more receptive to a lecture on the subject of sex than the subject of money.

Be honest with yourself about your financial predicament and do the things you don't like to do when it comes to your money matters. Get help by going to money workshops and debt consolidation counseling if you need it. It is time to do your financial statement, spending plan, balance your check book, clean up your credit, keep account of our daily spending and stop spending money you do not have. It is important to understand where you are financially so that you can prepare a road map as to where you want to go in the future with your money.

Wealth Chant

*I am open and honest about my money issues.*

Ain't know mountain high enough.

If you don't stand up for something you will fall for anything. Making a commitment to have higher standards when it come to the subject of money will not make you better than others, but will make you wiser. It is okay to want more out of life. We all have that innate desire to want to do more in order to get more out of life than enough. Be very careful that you do not let the money control you, but you learn to control the money.

Wealth Chant

*I choose a higher standard of living.*

Spending less = more quality of life.

Isn't it fun to be off the consumer bandwagon. Advertisers tell you that buying their item will make you happier, prettier, sexier and richer. Buying the item only made you poorer while making them richer. You tried to find happiness and a false sense of wealth accumulating a lot of stuff. Unfortunately, during the process you accumlated a lot of debt. Because of the "living like the Jones" mentality, you are more in debt and beholden to creditor like never before.The freedom of knowing that we do not owe anyone is true bliss and priceless. Take on a new attitude and choose to make the sacrifices that will get you out of credit card bondage.

Additionally, come to terms with realizing that the clothes, house or car do not make the man or the woman. Your identity is defined by how you perceive yourself and not by how others perceive you.

Wealth Chant

*I am happily frugal with my money.*

Stay-at-home Moms do work that can
never be adequately compensated.


Moms who stay at home get no respect. The work that Moms do is priceless. It is more challenging than running the White House. And still because there is no monetary compensation attach to this prestigious life choice, society assumes it is an extra-curricular activity. You and I know better. The sacrifices that Moms make today will create better leaders: more confident and compassionate beings who strive to make a better world.

Wealth Chant

*Moms work is priceless.*

Get more out of the money you make by eliminating the wants from your budget.

We all have a needs and wants list. Unfortunately, many of us think we need what we actually want. For example, many women believe they need to get their hair done once every two weeks. And they need a new dress to wear on a new date. Some men believe they need a new pair of golf clubs or Jordan sneakers to wear. If we want to become financially free it is so important that we get rid of the stuff in our lives and focus on the basic necessities for a period of time. Living below your means is a grand way to live a debt free life and sleep peacefully at night.

Wealth Chant

*I enjoy the basic necessities of life.*

Financial organization helps you see
what you are doing with your money.

So many of us are truly making a lot of money but we don't know where it is going. I read a story where a couple's combined income was $600,000 a year and they were living paycheck to paycheck. I am sure that you are thinking if I had that amount of money I would not have debt and would be home free. It is all relative. Most people who increase their income also increase their spending habits.

Sometimes people need help with getting their finances in order. Spending money can become an addiction too. Though it is legal and widely accepted by society, it will have you in the poor house no matter what your income level is if you do not control it. There are debt anonymous programs, financial advisors and money coaches that are willing to help.

Wealth Chant

*I am willing to reach out and get help with my finances.*

Million dollars is not a lot of money any more.

There was a time when you would be able to retire when you hit the millionaire status. Now, you still have to have a day job in order to live comfortably. The rate of inflation has caught up with the millionaire status. Let's dispel the myth about the avarice lifestyle of a millionaire. A millionaire today, lives in a middle class community, brought one house and paid it off, kept an economy car for no less than ten years, married to the same spouse and spend well below his/her means. Futhermore, millionaires invest a great deal of their income and save for a rainy day. They love life and retire at 65 with a nice nest egg. Lastly, they give back to the community as a volunteer and leave their inheritance to the ones they love hoping that they will continue the legacy.

Wealth Chant

*I want to live like a millionaire.*

Save your money, save your financial life.

Japanese people save a lot more than Americans. What we don't know is that the government encourages them to save by rationing their paycheck. For example, they are paid monthly. A monthly income forces you to budget. Second, they are paid a portion of their pay and given a bonus in a lump sum twice a year. Most Japanese people have developed a custom that the lump sum checks are put into a nest egg. Because the society as a whole encourages saving, they have a much higher saving ratio than Americans. In America, the motto is shop until you drop. We need to come to terms with the fact that we are going to have to become better savers. You can start to put away 10% of your income into a savings account. You should have it automatically deducted from your checking account to your savings each time you get paid. You will appreciate it when that rainy day comes because eventually it will rain.

Wealth Chant

*I patiently watch my money grow.*

Maturity begins on the day we accept
responsibility for our actions.

It is so easy to blame people and circumstances in our lives for why we haven't lived our purpose. It is my childhood upbringing, my violent marriage, the government, or God. To play the victim has us pointing the finger at someone else. When you point one finger at someone else, there are three fingers pointing back at you. Where you are right now in your life, you put yourself there. Develop an "if it is to be, it is up to me" mentality. By taking responsibility for your life, you can now take action to turn your life around for the better and put into action what it is you were divinely meant to do.

Wealth Chant

*I take responsibility for my actions.*

To know and not do is not yet to know.
*Zen saying*

Many people always say I know, but they will not do the work. If you are not willing to do the work and continue the destructive behavior, you do not know: For example, you know you need to lose weight but you keep on eating; you know you need to save money but you keep on spending. If you truly knew the benefits of something, you would be experiencing it. Give yourself the opportunity to know what it truly is like to live a life of wealth. You my have read about it. You may have dreamt about it. The only way you will know about a wealthy life is to go about the means of creating one for yourself.

Wealth Chant

**I am creating a wealthy lifestyle.**

What I know, I do. Find joy in your life work.

I love what I do! How many of you can say this about your life choices. It is a feeling of calm that brings joy to us and our joy permeates throughout the world. If everyone were blessed with this gift, the world would be a friendly exchange of our individual experience of love via our work.

Wealth Chant

*I work from a place of joy.*

Get out of the rat race and make your own piece of "cheese".

Too many people are trying to get ahead in the world of business by any means necessary. They throw caution to the wind and focus on winning the race. In the end, they may come out tired, defeated, and dejected. Even if they successfully accomplish their goal, they may have lost their soul in the process. Struggle is optional. You don't have to do negative acts to obtain wealth. You can do it the old fashion way. Give your very best. Be open and honest with those you do business with. Be dependable and consistent. Be patient. Your due diligence will pay off.

Wealth Chant

*I chose to do business morally and ethically.*

It is better to hire the expert than to be the expert.

Henry Ford had an eighth grade education. With the help of very smart people, he built the first affordable U. S. car that people still drive today. He may not have processed the aptitude to take on all the responsibility to run a major company but he had the wisdom to hire the right people who could. His work made him rich and helped million of folks enjoy the pleasure of driving.

Wealth Chant

*God grant me the wisdom to find the answers to all my life concerns.*

Ignorance is evil.
*African Proverb*

I remember the saying that ignorance is bliss, for whom? There is no liberation in being ignorant about life circumstances. You will pay big time for your inability to know what is going on in the money game. People will no doubt take advantage of you, if you choose to remain clueless about your finances. Even if you don't want to play in the money game, as long as you are in the world, you will be forced to be an involuntary participant.

Wealth Chant

**I am no longer ignorant about my money matters.**

Save money and money will save you.

*Famous Jamaican quote*

It is amazing that so many people go each day unprepared for the unexpected. They are the same people who will exclaim, "Why did this have to happen to me?" Whenever life's emergencies arise, it usually require money to solve the situation. This is one reason why we are on edge each day because we know we are unprepared for life lessons. Start saving money today. If it is $5 dollars per day from you lunch allowance, so be it. You will be at peace knowing there is money in the bank.

Wealth Chant

*I am saving my money each day.*

Money is emotional.

The one emotion that many people have about money is fear. Fear of not having enough money or fear that they will lose the money they have. There is one emotion we need to have about money today and that is to be at peace with money. This will not cost us a dime, but will bring many dimes to our aid because we are free to think of the good that money can bring into our life.

Use your money to bring more peace in the world. Give to a charity that promotes peace. Do not buy products that encourage war or hate. You have the power to make peace with your money and use your money to bring peace into your world.

Wealth Chant

*Money gives me peace of mind.*

My greatest fear is succumbing to my fears.

*Elon Bomani*

If I had succumbed to my fear of flying, I would have missed the beauty of the countries and people of Japan and Africa. I would not have played with the dolphins in Hawaii. If I had succumbed to my fear of public speaking, I would have missed the many people I have met, and they would have been denied the important message that I bring to aid their financial and wholistic living. If I had succumbed to my fear of success, I would have missed the joy of owning my own home and staying at home to raise my son. Fear stop dreams dead in their tracks. Don't let your fear contribute to you missing out on what life has to offer you.

Wealth Chant

**I face my fears courageously.**

You are prosperous when your life is filled
with peace, love and happiness.

Prosperous life is not defined by how much money you have. It is not something you acquire. It is something you have innately within you. It is an attitude of gratitude for the blessing that spirit has already given you. It's a choice to be happy, healthy, and wealthy.

Wealth Chant

*I live a prosperous life.*

The poor man and the rich man do not play together

*Ashanti proverb.*

How can someone poor teach you to be rich? They cannot. If you want to be like Oprah, you may want to study and practice some of the actions of a wealthy person. Just like everyone is unique and different, so is everyone's approach to living a wealthy lifestyle. You may create your own method but there are noticeable similarities that all rich people have. They become rich by thinking rich thoughts and doing rich deeds.

Wealth Chant

*I live a rich life.*

Millionaires tend to think alike.

Millionaires have many more challenges than the average person. They have many more risk taking skills. They have more failures. They have experienced more pain. On the other side, they have many more solutions to the challenges. Their risk gives them more rewards. Their failures bring them more success. Their pain brings them more opportunities to heal.

Wealth Chant

*I think like the wealthy.*

Networking improves your networth.

Networking will take you places. I can remember a sister healer who had called and ask if she could sell her book at a health conference I was giving. I was very glad to extend an opportunity for someone to make money. She had a great time, sold a couple of books and we kept in contact periodically. That was three years ago.

Recently, she was organizing a summit and called to give me an opportunity to do a workshop. It was a success and I generated leads for new clients and book sales. Networking for the sake of doing good will always bring good back to you. It may come from the party whom the good was done and it may not. Keep doing good work and blessings will show up someday in a very peculiar way.

Wealth Chant

*I network to increase my net worth.*

A balance life has a balanced check book.


Balance your checkbook. Stop writing bounced checks. Keep your account in order and in good standing. You will be asked for previous check statements when you want to buy a house, a business or a car. Lenders want to make sure you are being responsible with the money that they are lending you. If you are responsible and organized with your financial house, they will help you expand your financial wealth.


Wealth Chant


*I live a balance life with a balanced checkbook*

You must sell yourself.

When you do your own pubic relations, you are sometimes left with the feeling that you are prostituting your
way to success. This stems from the feeling of insecurity
that what I have to share is not important because I am
not important. What an erroneous thought. You cannot
have an idea unless God has given it to you. What you
are giving to the world is a service that people need.
You know that some people cannot live without this
information or product. Some people lives will change
dramatically when they come in contact with what you
have to offer.

Keep these thoughts at the forefront of your mind as you
go about the journey of sharing. You are not selling- you
are sharing. With this thought process; you can boldly
go where no woman/man has gone before.

Wealth Chant

*I sell to serve.*

You play an important small part in the big picture of life.

You are a unique person. There is no one like you. There is no one who can express life the way that you do. You have to hold that power to high esteem because it is of value to the world. If you were not an important part of life, Spirit would have not brought you here. There are no mistakes.

Wealth Chant

*What I have to share is of value.*

You can build a financial portfolio
with as little as $50 dollars a month.


So many people think that they have to be rich or need a lot of money to win the Wall Street game. This is not true. What is true, is that if you consistently invest a small sum of money in no-load, drip stocks over a 10 to 25 years, based on the history of the stock market, you are bound to accumulate a large sum of money. Wall Street may help you overcome the rate of inflation and give you a nice retirement plan. Investing no money at all, will guarantee you a poor lifestyle in your senior years.

Wealth Chant


*I am a successful Wall Street investor.*

The Earth bears fruits of many gifts.

All that we do in life on a daily basis is give and receive. I give my clients good advice that will heal their health challenges. I receive money in exchange. I give the money I received to the grocery store so that I can feed my family. The grocery store gives the money to the farmer in exchange for the produce. The farmer gives the money to his department store in exchange for clothes for his family. There is a harmonious exchange of activities that happens over the course of a day that brings us peace and the ability to take care of our living responsibilities. Let's enjoy the process.

Wealth Chant

*The abundant gifts of the earth help me to prosper.*

Out of simplicity come complete sanity.

Struggling in life is not natural, it is man made. It's the negative, ignorant thoughts of worry, anxiety, jealousy, greed, and envy that can make life complicated. Struggle usually occurs when we live above our means. We think that having a lot of stuff or doing a lot of things makes us an important person.

Life is truly simple. Living a simple life by choosing peace in all of our activities brings us so much joy. Our importance is not found in being humans doing, but in being human beings.

Wealth Chant

*I enjoy living a simple life.*

There's nothing to it, you can do  it.


No matter how difficult it may appear to achieve your dreams, you must just keep, keep'in on. You are spirit. You have within you the power to make mountains move and the ability to walk on water. Whatever you do, don't quit. Stay in the game. Give yourself an opportunity to take a break, step back and look at what is going on. You may need to make some changes. Get more information and have faith that God has another way to make what you desire come to be. Never believe that only a few are meant to live a grand life.

Wealth Chant

*My dreams come true.*

# Is Free Will free?

You have the free will to make all the choices in your life. With that freedom you must take responsibility for the negative and positive consequences of your choices. If you find yourself in financial bondage, remember, you put yourself there. It is your birthright to succeed and prosper.

Wealth Chant

*I chose to be financially free.*

Learn to work more effectively and efficiently with the money you have.

There was an old woman who worked in a laundry shop for a living. She saved a portion of her income over the course of 60 years and donated thousands of dollars to a college to help underprivileged youth get a higher education. Who would have thought that a woman with a very modest income could save a large sum of money. The amount that she gave was equivalent to what millionaires give. Everyone was in shock and surprise that she had the strength and persistence to save that large amount of money. She was given awards and became well known around the world for her caring deed. This act was priceless and left an indelible mark on our consciousness that we could do even more with our money.

Wealth Chant

*I do good with the money I make.*

Knowledge is better than riches. *Cameroon proverb*

Many of the wealthy, famous people we know today have stories of acquiring wealth and losing it, and acquiring wealth again. If you have the knowledge of how you obtained the wealth, even if you loose it because the stock market crash, or you made a bad business deal, the knowledge didn't die with the circumstances. Financial knowledge stays with you forever. And with knowledge, if you fall, you have the intellect to acquire riches again and the wisdom to increase its staying power.

Wealth Chant

*I am knowledgeable about money and how it can create a rich life for me.*

If it don't make dollars, it don't make sense.

Why work for free? Who can afford to work for free? Many people when they start a business charge very low fees because they are afraid to ask for what they are worth. You have to be willing to accept money into your life without thinking you are prostituting for it. Be reasonable. If you have the skills that are in demand and you know you can serve people well, get the top dollar you deserve. If they will not pay you the money, they will surely pay someone else who knows their worth.

Wealth Chant

*I value my worth.*

www.**thedynamicdiva**.com

Little by little grow the Banana.
*Zaire proverb*

You have heard the quote Rome was not built in a day and neither will your business or your financial picture change over night as you start to implement actions on these formidable endeavors. Take your time and keep your eye on the prize. You will have to patient, persistent and use prudence as you travel this road. It may seem so far in the future, you cannot see the forest for the trees. Just keep in mind that the tree is planted and it is growing and awaiting your arrival.

Wealth Chant

**I am patient, practical and persistent
with my business dreams and goals.**

Buying a bigger home and car will not bring you happiness when you are stressed out about how you are going to pay the monthly note for them.

It is so important that we all live within our means. Even though we purchase things on credit many of us forget we will have to pay the money back and with interest. Think long and hard before you make that big purchase. Can you really afford it? Have you set up your retirement plan? Is your emergency fund in place? Or are you trying to live like the Jones on Joe income?

Wealth Chant

*I happily live within my means.*

Give your children love and security
before you give them money.

A very confident, secure, loving child will be successful in life no matter how much money they have. When
children feel the power of being accepted for who and
what they are, no matter what actions they take, they will
blossom right before your eyes. Tiger Woods and the
Williams sisters achieved great success because their
parents (someone stayed at home) were their for them
every step of the way and had their best interest at heart.
They built character, morals and values that surpass any
monetary or sport accolades that they have received.
And when their career is over, they will have the foundation to be successful in any personal or professional
endeavor they choose-because a loving foundation was
set for them at the very beginning.

Wealth Chant

*I give my children an abundance of love.*

The bless'in is in the lesson.

Failure is not failure when it is a lesson that assists you in accomplishing your future dreams and goals. My son never failed at walking. When he would fall after taking his first steps, he knew at a young age that falling was a necessary process for him to grow into a champion walker. He never got discouraged or frustrated. Matter of fact, he gave his falling no power because he focus all of his attention on walking-the blessing. He walks beautifully now and has included running, skipping and jumping to his repertoire. You once had that same nonchalant attitude. It's now time to return to the thought of taking each new task (that appears insurmountable), and accept learning lesson (failure) as a necessary means to a successful end. It's just a matter of time before a successful outcome will be born. You just have to keep your eye on the prize!

Wealth Chant

*I am blessed with many lessons.*

# Mind your own Business.

Many people think that when they own a business they will not be tied down with the boring task of bookkeeping and accounting for the business. They say they will leave the responsibility of the money to their hired help, their financial planner, accountant or the bookkeeper. This is a BIG MISTAKE. When you are left in the dark about your business financial matter, you are setting yourself up for someone to take advantage of your ignorance of money matters. They will only help themselves to your money. Nobody is going to take care of your money better than you. Tony Robbins made that mistake and lost $381,000 because he was not paying attention to where his money was going. Ignorance about money matters can be very costly.

## Wealth Chant

*I am minding my own business.*

Mom, can I have the dump truck? I'll pay you back.
*Rriiver Nyile 2 years old*

Children need to start learning about money as soon as they can talk. You will be doing them a disservice by thinking that when they are very young they are not ready to learn about a complicated matter such as money. Money is no more complicated then saying 1 +1 is 2. Besides, it is an easy way to introduce them to math by discussing money with them on a daily basis.

Wealth Chant

**I will teach young people about dollars and cents.**

Have the unmitigated guile, and the audacity to dream big dreams and make them come true.

Can you say I can have everything and honestly believe it? You are put on notice to have more conviction for your good. Society teaches us that we live in scarcity, that there is not enough to go around. So we convince ourselves that we can have a little piece of pie. You need to believe you can have the whole pie and enjoy it without any guilt, shame or feeling that you are being greedy. There is plenty in the universal world. There is enough for each of us to release our dreams and more. We just need to believe it in order to achieve it.

Wealth Chant

*I dare to make my big dreams come true.*

You work so much harder and longer
when you do it to pay the bills.

When we are doing work that is not our purpose and bring in slave wages, we feel as though it is an arduous task. When we do a task year in and out, it becomes very stressful and unfulfilling. Our body reminds us that the job does not fit us when we start to get aches and pains. Then we start calling in sick too often. This is a sure sign that our job is making us sick. Our attitude at the job becomes contagious and we start to make other people sick. We need to find the work that makes us feel good and does good in the world.

Wealth Chant

*I seek a great job that seeks me.*

# Play the game of life.

You have got to play at life. Kids learn by way of pretending and using their imagination. We adults become more productive by pretending and using our imagination. So, let's return to playing at life. Sometimes, I pretend to be a Mom. Other times, I pretend to be a wife. Often times, I have a lot of fun pretending to be a businesswoman and an author. By pretending, I do not take life very serious. I do not need to be perfect or know all the answers. I enjoy the process and the adventure of seeing how it will all work itself out with a positive attitude. I know that a positive attitude is strength of the imagination when we live in such a negative world. Even so, when I use my imagination, the world is positive and a joy to (save) experience.

Wealth Chant

*I enjoy playing the game called life.*

Exercise is meditation in motion.

I suffered from this affliction. I never had time for exercise. To truly have a wealth of health you have got to include exercise in you daily plan. It is a great cleanser and detoxifier for the body. Moreover, you create endorphins from the brain (hormone that make you feel good) that relaxes the body and gets rid of the stress. When you expend the negative energy, you make room for more peace and the positive energy that will bring you fantastic ideas and more good fortune into your life. So, get out and get some Vitamin D (sunshine), fresh air and have a great walk. It will do wonders for your mind, body and spirit.

Wealth Chant

*I have a wealth of health.*

# Become a do-it –yourself person.

I get so much more gratification from the work I do for myself. I feel that I am in control of my destiny. And I can determine were my life is going. Yes, you can do it too.  Instead of finding a part time job, you should start a small business to supplement your income. You can get more pleasure from the work you do for yourself. The business will make you more money and provide many tax write-offs that a part-time job cannot do. Moreover, a business will allow you to express your unique talents and facilitate greater opportunity for growth and development. At a job, you are helping someone else realize their dreams and make them wealthy. With a business, you are in charge of your life. You decide how long you work, where you work and with whom you work.

Wealth Chant

*I earn great money from the work I do all by myself.*

You are success waiting to happen.

You've got what it takes to do some phenomenal things. It is all inside of you waiting anxiously to come out and express itself. You know deep down inside you are success waiting to happen. It is now time to get moving and grooving. Wake up the success giant inside of you and let the world be made better for it! BAM

Wealth Chant

*I successfully accomplish my desires.*

Melancholy, mundane life leads to mediocrity.

Why are you allowing Michael Jordan, Tiger Woods, Tony Robbins and Katie Couric have all the fun? If you sometimes find yourself reading the gossip columns and living vicariously through someone else's life, it is a sure sign that nothing exciting or interesting is going on in your own life. This is pathetic. Get a life. When you are happy and on purpose, you don't care nor have the time to figure out what is going on in the life of others. You need to stop watching T.V., get out of the bleacher seats and start dancing on the front stage of your life. You are the star of your life.

Wealth Chant

*I am the star of my life.*

For unto every one that hath shall be given, and he shall have abundance: but from him that hath not shall be taken away even that which he hath. *Mt. 25:29 King James Version*

What you don't use, you will lose. If you have God given talents that you are neglecting, your talents will be wasted. It is not a punishment from God. You can't blame God for your inability to use the gifts given to you. It is all up to you. By not using the gift, abundance becomes an out of reach dream. When the gifts are used to honor and bless others, the blessings will return to you tenfold. So, stop procrastinating: dust off the guitar and finish that number one song; pull out the pots and pans and complete the recipe book; and reopen that manuscript and submit the next best seller. You and, only you, can make your dreams come true.

Wealth Chant

*I will finish all the projects I start.*

It's not about living a perfect life,
but more about improving your life.


We are all success in progress. So many people stop producing their life's work because they think it should be perfect. They think they should not have any failures, setback or defeats. Please. When did we become so perfect that we stop being realistic? There is no such thing as perfection. We can improve on circumstance, but there is no utopic way of achieving success. It is always good to strive to do better, but sometime it is okay to be content with just doing a good job.


Wealth Chant


*I am improving each day.*

Small people can grow up to do big business.

I have taken my son on real estate closings, to small claim court hearings, the bank and on many other business errands. I inform all of my peers that he is my "administrative assistant". No, it does not follow business etiquette, as we know it. Even so, it is time to make a change and people can still do a great job of business when they have their children involved. My child has been a great addition to our family. I have been able to successfully run a business and raise my son to be a great little person. In Africa, they allow children to run around the floor of the parliament. They understand that parents will perform successful tasks when they can bring their kids to work. Maybe children cannot be at all work places, but there are businesses that can create circumstances that will allow women/men to work and raise their children.

Wealth Chant

*I can run a successful business while raising my child.*

Children don't need your money as
much as the need your T-I-M-E.

You have heard of the quote time is money. The amount
of money you make and save will either give or take
away time. It may even save you time in the long run. For
many parents, the goal is to find the career that will allow
us to spend more time with our children. Time with the
family is priceless, especially the moments that will only
happen once—the first crawl, walk or talk. The reason
why we work so hard is so that we have more time to do
the things we want to do. Do you think you have to work
a forty-hour or more work week? There are careers out
there that will allow you to spend more time with your
child. Try a stay at home-business, like network marketing, that will help you develop residual income, which
over time will have you work less and make more money
by using other people efforts.

Wealth Chant

*I am willing to find the career that will
allow me to spend more time with family.*

Those who give away their treasure wisely,
giveth away their plagues: they that retain
their increase, heap up sorrow.
*Egyptian Proverb*

If you are having a down day, it means you are not doing enough for someone else. The best way to feel better about yourself is to help someone feel better about themselves. Do you have a charity that you give to? When you do find one, give your time, money, or your used clothes that you haven't worn in ten years. Someone will appreciate the attention. You will feel good about doing some philanthropic work. Philanthropy is not only enjoyed by the rich, but can be enjoyed by you too.

Wealth Chant

**My treasures help some one in need.**

Labor not after riches first, and think thou afterwards will enjoy them. She who neglects the present moment, throws away all that she hath.

*Egyptian Proverb*

You have to enjoy a rich life now before the money shows up. It is not the end result of acquiring masses of money that make you happy. It is the rewards along the journey that makes the trip worthwhile. It is in knowing that you had the utmost integrity about your approach towards wealth. It is about not compromising your family and your health to acquire it. It is about giving away some of your blessings to enrich someone else life. It is about sharing your experiences to help someone else achieve the same.

Wealth Chant

**The rewards along the journey gives me a rich life.**

Do not lend money unless you can give it away.

There was a woman that needed to pay her rent on time or she was going to get evicted from her home. The woman's niece gave her a sad story about how she needed to borrow her aunt's rent money to get out of this crisis. The niece promised to pay her back the money before her rent was due. Her rent day came and passed and the niece never showed up with the rent money. The woman was evicted from her home and she was force to live in a home that was less favorable. The moral of this story is, if you don't have money that you can live without, don't loan it to anyone. You will be the one to truly suffer if you cannot take care of the basics.

Wealth Chant

*Charity begins with me.*

I was so po, I could not even afford the or.

There was a time in my life when we were on welfare. I can remember praying for the first of the month to come. I can remember fasting involuntarily. I can remember looking in the cabinet and finding absolutely nothing to eat. This is my past history with money. Today, I understand that my past circumstances do not have a reflection on what I can accomplish today. In my mind, I understand that today is a new day and I can trade in my poor childhood for a wealthy adulthood.

Wealth Chant

*Today abundance is mine.*

I lot of people become adults but many have never become grown up.

*Elon Bomani*

Many adults are afraid to take responsibility for their financial condition. Many have become adults but still are childlike in how they treat money. They are looking for a parent to take care of them. When they were young it was mom and dad. When they became older their surrogate parent was the job, welfare system or government contract subsidized services. Adults acquired the money but never took the baby steps to grow into learning about the power of money. I don't have time. I don't want to be rich. I don't have any money to save. All are excuses they gave themselves. So when the bottom fell from beneath them, they lost their savings, secure job, and wanted to blame somebody else for their circumstances. A person who matures and becomes a grownup knows that they are responsible for their financial circumstance. They are willing to seek out the necessary education to increase their economic standing and create new means of acquiring money to share with family, friends and associates. They understand that they are the rightful heirs to the abundance that life has to offer and are willing to do the necessary work to empower themselves.

Wealth Chant

***I chose to grow into my wealth by taking resposibilityfor my financial state.***

It is honour to thy nature when worthily employed, when thou directs it to wrong purposes, it shameth and destroy thee.

*Egyptian Proverb*

What we do with the money in our lives determines our true understanding of its power. If we use money to buy drugs, sex, or alcohol to help us escape life's predicaments, it will become very elusive. If you notice that people who use money in that manner never can hold on to it, find it, or they lose it often. Money has a way of leaving us when it is not serving a higher purpose.

Wealth Chant

***I honor the power of money.***

Money and I are not on speaking terms.

Many people have a love/hate relationship with money. When you hate money or the people who have money, you repel money from you. Money in and of itself has no personality. What we think about money and do with money will only bring to light its good or its bad. If you let go of your fears about money with positive loving thought about money, money will bring many blessings into your life. Money is neither good nor bad, it is your thought about money that makes it so.

Wealth Chant

*Money is an expression of love.*

*Your personalize chant page*

(Make up your own chants that works for you)

_____

_____

_____

_____

_____

_____

_____

_____

_____

_____

_____

_____

_____

*Your personalize chant page*

(Make up your own chants that works for you)

_____

_____

_____

_____

_____

_____

_____

_____

_____

_____

_____

_____

_____

_____

_____

# Your personalize chant page

## (Make up your own chants that works for you)

_____

_____

_____

_____

_____

_____

_____

_____

_____

_____

_____

_____

_____

_____

_____

www.**thedynamicdiva**.com

# Negative Chants **VS**. Positive Chants

Money doesn't grow on trees

*Money flows to me from various sources*

A day late and a dollar short

*I have more than enough money*

Pinching Pennies

*I handle money well*

Robbing Peter to pay Paul

*I am fair, moral and ethical with my money*

Money burns a hole in his pocket

*I save and invest my money wisely*

Money is the root of all evil

*Money is an expression of love*

# Recommended Readings

One Minute Millionare by Mark Victor Hansen & Robert G. Allen (Harmony Books, 2002)

The Writings of Florence Scovel Shinn by Florence Scovel Shinn (Devorss Publication,1988)

Creating Money by Sanaya Roman & Duane Packer (H J Kramer, 1988)

# Suggested Website

www.thedynamicdiva.com-Daily inspiration

Inspiring women to become more healthy,wealthy and wise!

# Suggested Workshop

The Dynamic Diva Dollars Wealth Workshop

Coming January 2008-check for futher information at www.thedynamicdiva.com

# Suggested AudioCD

Wealth Chant
Order at www.thedynamicdiva.com or call 281.778.9416